The Story of Christmas

with Scripture

Retold by Jill Wolf

**Illustrated by Jean Rudegeair
and Nancy Herndon**

**Copyright © 1986 Antioch Publishing Company
ISBN 0-89954-459-2
Made in the United States of America**

 Antioch Publishing Company
Yellow Springs, Ohio 45387

Long ago in a little town called Nazareth, there lived a young woman named Mary. She had promised to marry a carpenter named Joseph. One day an angel appeared to Mary.

"Do not be afraid," he told her. "God is pleased with you. You will have a baby boy and call Him Jesus. He will be the Son of God and the Savior of the world."

Although Mary did not understand how all this could happen, she bowed her head to show that she would do as God wished.

"Do not be afraid, Mary, for you have found favor with God."
Luke 1:30

The angel also told Mary that her cousin Elizabeth was going to have a baby, too. Mary went to visit Elizabeth so they could share their joy.

When Mary came in her house, Elizabeth knew, through God's Spirit, that Mary's baby was going to be the Son of God. "Blessed are you among women!" cried Elizabeth.

"My soul praises God," said Mary, "for all He has done!"

"Blessed are you among women, and blessed is the fruit of your womb!"

Luke 1:42

When Mary returned home, Joseph found out she was going to have a baby. He didn't know if he should marry her. Then an angel appeared to Joseph in a dream.

"Joseph, don't be afraid to take Mary as your wife," the angel told him. "The child she carries is from the Holy Spirit. You shall call the child Jesus, and He will save people from their sins."

So Mary and Joseph were soon married and waited anxiously for the birth of the baby.

...behold, an angel of the Lord appeared to him in a dream, saying..."And she will bring forth a Son, and you shall call His name JESUS, for He will save His people from their sins."
Matthew 1:20,21

As Mary's time to give birth drew near, the Roman rulers of the Jews in Judea decided to count all the people. Everyone had to go to the town where he had been born to be counted for a special tax.

Since Joseph was from Bethlehem, he and Mary had to leave Nazareth and travel the long road to Joseph's hometown.

It was a hard journey, especially for Mary, because her baby was due at any time. The long trip made her very tired.

And Joseph also went…to be registered with Mary, his betrothed wife, who was with child.

Luke 2: 4,5

Many people had come to Bethlehem to be counted and the city was crowded. When Mary and Joseph arrived, all the inns were full. They had no place to stay!

One kindly innkeeper saw how tired and worried they were. "There's no room at the inn," he told them, "but you can sleep in the stable out back."

So Joseph and Mary stayed in the stable where the animals ate and slept.

...there was no room for them in the inn.
Luke 2:7

Inside the stable there was only straw for Mary and Joseph to lie on, but they didn't mind. They were glad to have shelter on a cold night, especially with a baby on the way.

While the gentle cows and sheep looked on, Mary gave birth to her baby. She wrapped Him in soft, warm clothes and laid Him in a manger full of hay from which the animals ate their food. It made a cozy bed for the Baby Jesus.

The hearts of Mary and Joseph were filled with wonder and joy over the birth of Jesus. Everything had happened just as God said.

And she...wrapped Him in swaddling cloths, and laid Him in a manger...

Luke 2:7

On a hillside near Bethlehem, several shepherds were watching their flocks that night. Suddenly an angel appeared before them and a great light shone around them. The shepherds were frightened.

But the angel said to them, "Do not be afraid. I bring you good news which will give joy to all people. Today your Savior has been born in Bethlehem."

Then more angels appeared and they all praised God, singing: "Glory to God in the highest, and on earth peace, good will toward men."

"…behold, I bring you good tidings of great joy which will be to all people."

Luke 2:10

When the angels were gone, the shepherds said to one another, "Let us go to Bethlehem and see the Savior that the Lord has told us about."

They hurried to Bethlehem and searched for the Baby Jesus. Finally they found Him in the stable, lying in the manger, just as the angel had said.

After the shepherds had seen Jesus, they went out and told everyone they met about this very special child. Then the shepherds returned to tend their flocks, praising God for what they had heard and seen that night.

And they came with haste and found Mary and Joseph, and the Babe lying in a manger.

Luke 2:16

After Jesus was born, wise men from the East came to Jerusalem looking for Him. They had travelled far on their camels, guided by a very bright star.

"Where is the King of the Jews?" they asked King Herod of Judea. "We have seen His star in the East and have come to worship Him."

Herod asked his counselors, then told the wise men, "Go to Bethlehem. When you have found the Child, bring back word so I can go to worship Him, too."

… wise men from the East came to Jerusalem, saying, "… we have seen His star in the East and have come to worship Him."

Matthew 2:1,2

The wise men followed the star to Bethlehem until it came to stand over the house where Jesus stayed. They went in and found Him with His mother Mary.

As the wise men knelt down before Jesus, they gave Him gifts fit for a king—gold, frankincense, and a sweet perfume called myrrh.

In a dream God warned the wise men not to tell King Herod where Jesus was. Herod didn't like the idea of another king and meant to harm Jesus. So the wise men went home by a different way.

Mary and Joseph, the shepherds, and the wise men celebrated the birth of Jesus on that first Christmas. And we also celebrate Christmas because it is Jesus' birthday.

Just as the wise men gave Jesus gifts, we exchange gifts. We share the joy of the good news of God's love for us, just as the shepherds did.

God loved us so much that He gave us the best Christmas present of all—His only Son. And we can give Jesus the best birthday present of all—remembering that Christmas is His birthday.

For God so loved the world that He gave His only begotten Son…
John 3:16

THE END